INFIELDERS

By Jason Glaser

Gareth Stevens
Publishing

Please visit our Web site, www.garethstevens.com. For a free color catalog of all our high-quality books, call toll free 1-800-542-2595 or fax 1-877-542-2596.

Library of Congress Cataloging-in-Publication Data

Glaser, Jason.
Infielders / Jason Glaser.
     p. cm. — (Play ball. Baseball)
Includes index.
ISBN 978-1-4339-4488-8 (pbk.)
ISBN 978-1-4339-4489-5 (6-pack)
ISBN 978-1-4339-4487-1 (library binding)
1. Fielding (Baseball)—Juvenile literature. 2. Infielders (Baseball)—Juvenile literature. I. Title.
GV870.G53 2011
796.357'24—dc22

                          2010026667

First Edition

Published in 2011 by
Gareth Stevens Publishing
111 East 14th Street, Suite 349
New York, NY 10003

Designer: Haley W. Harasymiw
Editor: Greg Roza

Photo credits: Cover, p. 1 Doug Benc/Getty Images; (cover, back cover, pp. 2–3, 5, 11, 15, 35, 42–48 background image on all), pp. 40, 41, 43 Shutterstock.com; pp. 4, 35 Al Bello/Getty Images; p. 5 Chuck Solomon/Sports Illustrated/Getty Images; p. 6 Blank Archives/Getty Images; p. 7 Buyenlarge/Getty Images; pp. 8, 9 Mark Rucker/Transcendental Graphics/Getty Images; p. 10 Chris Hondros/Newsmakers/Getty Images; p. 11 Keystone/Archive Photos/Getty Images; p. 12 Photo File/Getty Images; p. 13 Stephen Dunn/Getty Images; p. 14 Scott Halleran/ Getty Images; p. 15 David Ake/AFP/Getty Images; p. 17 Al Messerschmidt/Getty Images; p. 18 Don Smith/MLB Photos/Getty Images; p. 19 Fred Vuich/Sports Illustrated/Getty Images; p. 20 Abelimages/Getty Images; p. 21 Ronald C. Modra/Sports Imagery/Getty Images; p. 22 Jeff Gross/Getty Images; p. 23 Kevin C. Cox/Getty Images; p. 24 Mark Cunningham/ MLB Photos/Getty Images; p. 25 Tom DiPace/Sports Illustrated/Getty Images; pp. 26, 37 Jed Jacobsohn/Getty Images; p. 27 Bob Levey/Getty Images; p. 28 Bruce Kluckhohn/ Getty Images; p. 29 Focus on Sport/Getty Images; p. 30 Ron Vesley/MLB Photos/Getty Images; p. 31 Joe Robbins/Getty Images; p. 32 Drew Hallowell/Getty Images; p. 33 Brad Mangin/ MLB Photos/Getty Images; pp. 34, 36, 38, 44 Otto Greule Jr./Getty Images; p. 39 Ezra Shaw/ Getty Images; p. 42 iStockphoto.com; p. 45 Hulton Archive/Getty Images.

Printed in the United States of America

CPSIA compliance information: Batch #CW11GS: For further information contact Gareth Stevens, New York, New York at 1-800-542-2595.

CONTENTS

Boldface words appear in the glossary.

THE RUN STOPPERS

Baseball infielders are the four players who guard against runners trying to make it around the bases to score. Stopping base runners is the biggest part of playing defense.

A Tight Spot

On August 23, 2009, the Philadelphia Phillies led the New York Mets 9–6 in the ninth **inning**. The Mets scored a run—making the score 9–7—and had runners on first base and second base. The next batter for the Mets could bring in three runs and win the game. The Phillies needed three outs to win.

Jimmy Rollins of the Phillies makes a play to Eric Bruntlett against the New York Mets.

4

Phillies second baseman Eric Bruntlett was moving into position when the ball was hit toward him. Bruntlett caught it, putting the batter out. This meant the two Mets runners needed to get back to the bases they started from. Bruntlett stepped on second base to get one runner out and **tagged** out the other. It was an unassisted **triple play**—Bruntlett made all three outs himself! This was just the fifteenth unassisted triple play in major league history.

The unassisted triple play might be rare, but it shows just how exciting playing the infield can be. Read on to learn more about what it takes to make big infield plays.

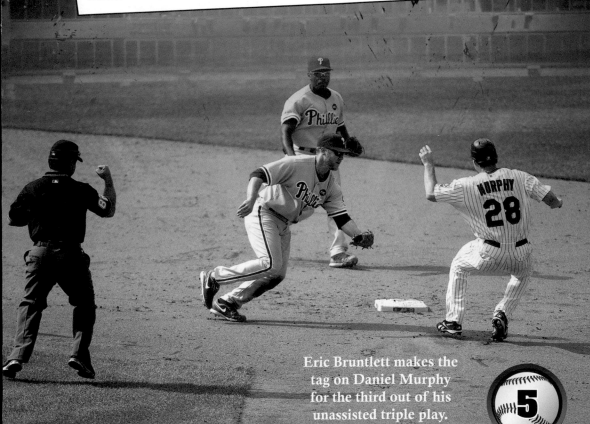

Eric Bruntlett makes the tag on Daniel Murphy for the third out of his unassisted triple play.

5

Rise of the Basemen

Baseball grew out of two games: cricket and rounders. Cricket is a British sport where players hit a small ball with a flat bat. Rounders is a child's game. Today, baseball is a fun game for both kids and adults.

Room for Everyone

Anybody wanting to play ball in the 1800s could play in the field. Some early baseball games had as many as 50 people on defense! The ball was soft and light, so people played without gloves. Since the soft ball didn't fly very far, it was thrown from player to player to move it around. The defense actually hit runners with the ball between bases for outs!

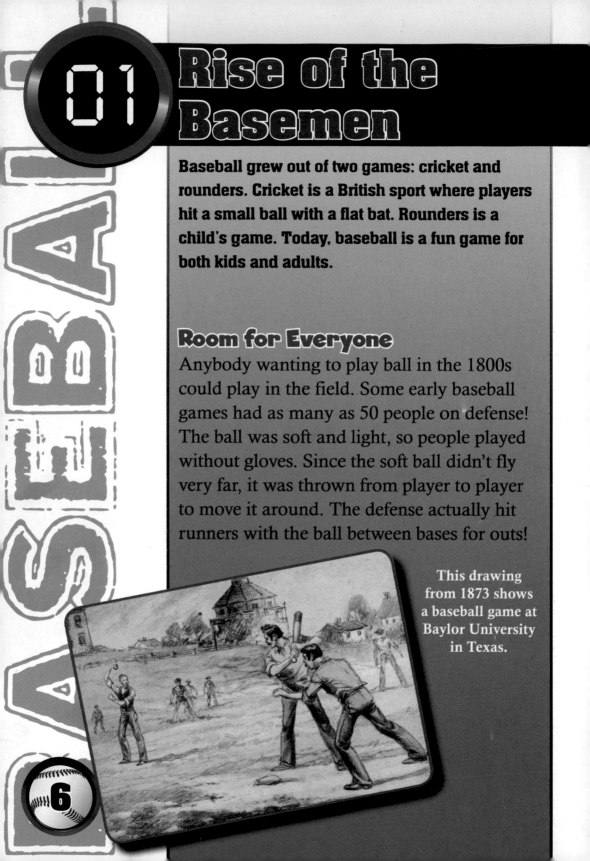

This drawing from 1873 shows a baseball game at Baylor University in Texas.

BASEBALL

In 1845, a group of players from New York City formed the first organized baseball team—the Knickerbockers. They established the first set of rules and created the diamond-shaped infield. They also decided that the defense could not get outs by hitting runners with the ball anymore. Instead, fielders had to tag runners with the ball between bases. Runners could also be "thrown out" at a base. To do this, an infielder had to touch a base with his foot while catching the ball before the runner reached the base. These new rules meant that infielders needed to position themselves near the bases to stop runners.

The term "knickerbocker" comes from a type of short pants—knickers—worn by the Dutch, who settled the area that became New York City. The first Knickerbocker baseball team may have taken the name from the Knickerbocker Engine Company, a volunteer fire department.

In 1858, the ball was changed to a harder one made with a rubber core wrapped in yarn and covered with leather. It was much like a modern baseball. This ball traveled farther when hit and could be thrown farther. Players could get the ball to each other with one throw, which meant fewer players were needed on defense.

The newer baseballs were much harder than the original balls. Many players began wearing padded gloves, like the one shown on page 9, on their catching hands.

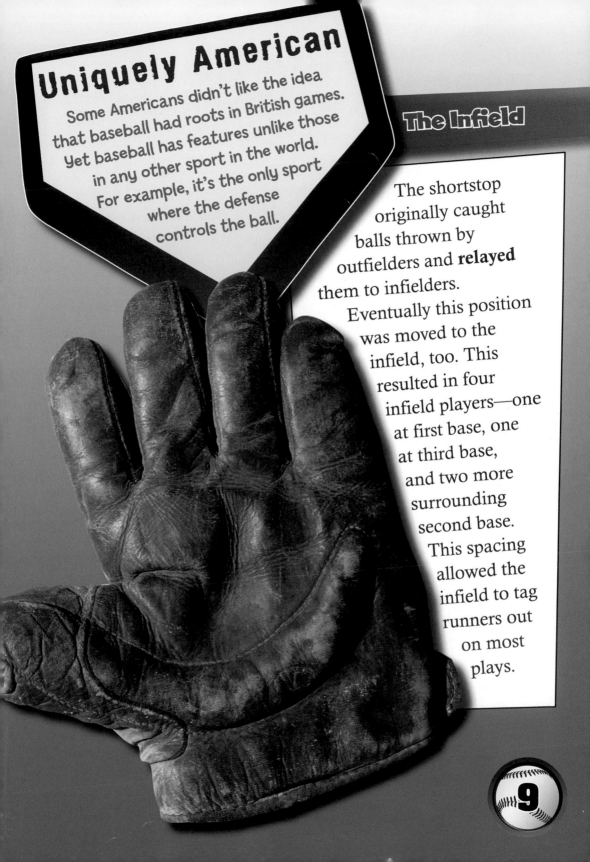

Uniquely American

Some Americans didn't like the idea that baseball had roots in British games. Yet baseball has features unlike those in any other sport in the world. For example, it's the only sport where the defense controls the ball.

The shortstop originally caught balls thrown by outfielders and **relayed** them to infielders. Eventually this position was moved to the infield, too. This resulted in four infield players—one at first base, one at third base, and two more surrounding second base. This spacing allowed the infield to tag runners out on most plays.

9

The speed and excitement of running the bases and throwing runners out is a large part of why Americans love baseball. Here are some of the infielders whose gloves, arms, and feet helped cement baseball as "America's pastime."

The Flying Dutchman

The greatest shortstop in baseball played more than over 100 years ago. Honus Wagner's giant hands grabbed any ball that came his way, and his long arms threw right on target every time. After a 21-year career that lasted from 1897 to 1917, Wagner was among the first players **inducted** into the Baseball Hall of Fame, which opened in 1936.

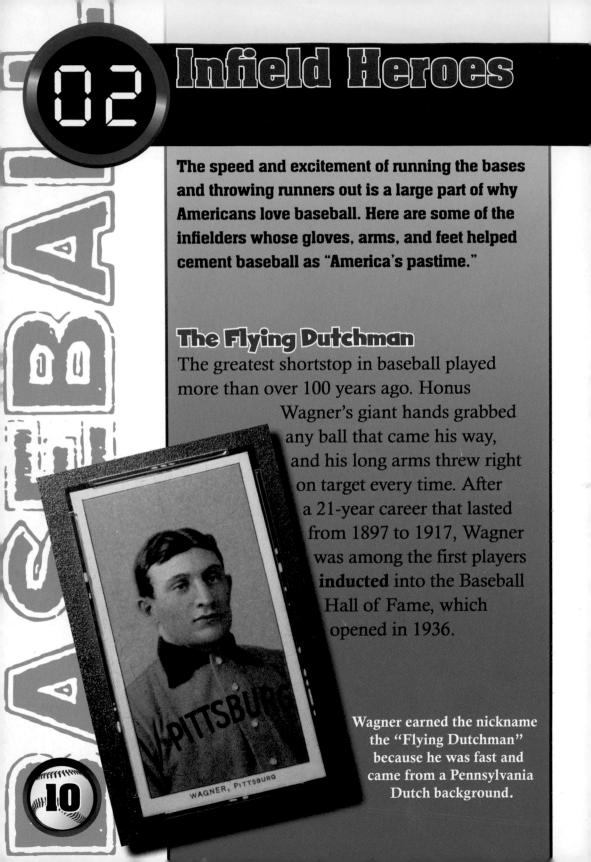

Wagner earned the nickname the "Flying Dutchman" because he was fast and came from a Pennsylvania Dutch background.

WAGNER, PITTSBURG

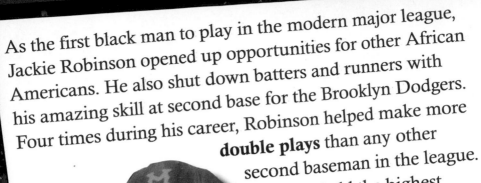

As the first black man to play in the modern major league, Jackie Robinson opened up opportunities for other African Americans. He also shut down batters and runners with his amazing skill at second base for the Brooklyn Dodgers. Four times during his career, Robinson helped make more **double plays** than any other second baseman in the league. He also held the highest **fielding percentage** for a second baseman with at least 150 games.

Robinson played in six World Series and helped the Dodgers become World Champions in 1955.

Baltimore Orioles third baseman Brooks Robinson is one of the few Hall of Famers remembered more for defense than for hitting. For 23 seasons between 1955 and 1977, Robinson dominated the infield area between third base and shortstop. He won 16 **Gold Glove** Awards in a row and an MVP (most valuable player) award for the 1970 World Series. His ability to snatch balls out of the air and grab hard-hit **line drives** earned him the nickname the "Human Vacuum Cleaner."

Brooks Robinson prepares to catch a line drive.

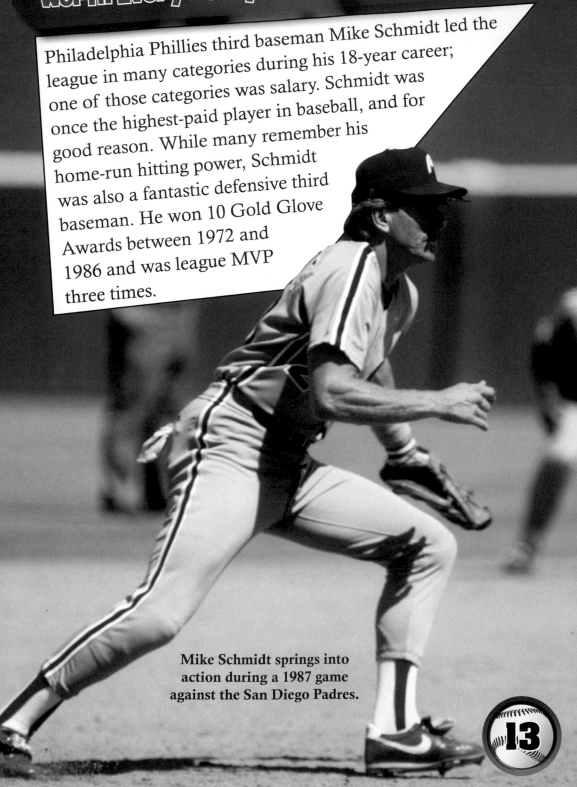

Philadelphia Phillies third baseman Mike Schmidt led the league in many categories during his 18-year career; one of those categories was salary. Schmidt was once the highest-paid player in baseball, and for good reason. While many remember his home-run hitting power, Schmidt was also a fantastic defensive third baseman. He won 10 Gold Glove Awards between 1972 and 1986 and was league MVP three times.

Mike Schmidt springs into action during a 1987 game against the San Diego Padres.

The Wizard

The energetic shortstop Ozzie Smith often did backflips on the field after making great plays. Smith "flipped out" for 19 years, from 1978 to 1996, mostly for the St. Louis Cardinals. He was a Gold Glove winner 13 times in a row. His speed let him get balls others couldn't, including one in 1986 where he leaped over a slower teammate to catch the ball. Smith's amazing skill earned him the nickname the "Wizard."

Donnie Baseball

Don Mattingly

First baseman Don Mattingly—popularly known as "Donnie Baseball"—never won a World Series in his 14-year career with the New York Yankees. However, from 1982 to 1995, he was one of baseball's best infielders. His career fielding percentage (.996) is among the highest in baseball history for longtime players. He also won nine Gold Glove Awards thanks to his consistent play.

Two-time Gold Glove shortstop and third baseman Cal Ripken Jr. played more than 3,000 games—and 2,632 of them were in a row. On September 6, 1995, Ripken tied legend Lou Gehrig's record of 2,131 games in row. In 2002, baseball fans voted that day as the most memorable event in baseball history. His entire career, from 1981 to 2001, was spent with his hometown Baltimore Orioles team.

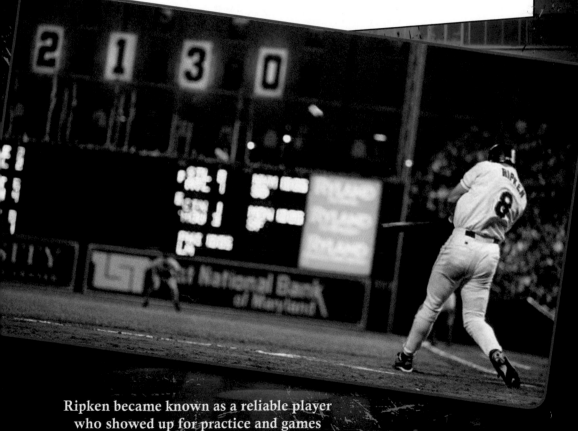

Ripken became known as a reliable player who showed up for practice and games despite minor injuries. These qualities earned him the nickname "Iron Man."

After a batter hits the ball, infielders try to get it as quickly as possible. Fast action helps keep the other team from getting bases and runs—or even from getting on base at all!

The Four Infielders

A baseball diamond is marked by four bases set on a patch of dirt and sand. The batter hits from a flat base called home plate. The other three bases, which are like stuffed bags, mark the base paths that the batter runs around after hitting a ball. A team's four infielders are positioned around these bases.

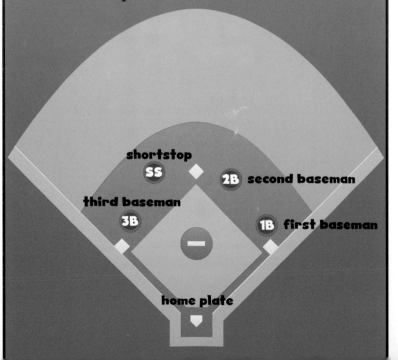

shortstop
SS

2B second baseman

third baseman
3B

1B first baseman

home plate

Tampa Bay Rays shortstop Jason Bartlett makes a throw to first base after snagging a low, bouncing ball.

First Line of Defense

Infielders try to keep the ball from getting into the grassy area, or outfield, behind them. They also need to get the ball to the bases ahead of any runners. If an infielder catches the ball before it hits the ground, the runner is out immediately. If the ball hits the ground, the team must get it to an infielder who will try to tag the runner out or step onto the base before the runner can get to it for a **force-out**.

Hitters run toward first base after hitting a **fair ball**. If the first baseman gets the ball and touches first base before the hitter does, the runner is out. The first baseman is very important because of the high number of throws made to first base following hit balls.

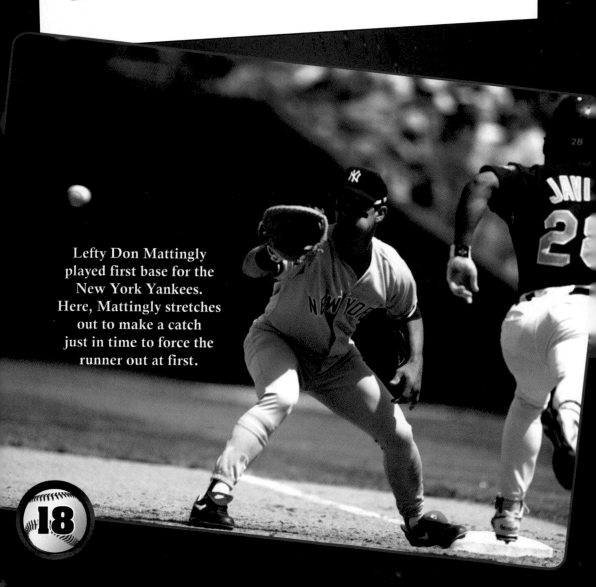

Lefty Don Mattingly played first base for the New York Yankees. Here, Mattingly stretches out to make a catch just in time to force the runner out at first.

Left-Hand Advantage

Many teams use left-handed players at first base because they catch with the glove on their right hand. This lets them stand on the base and reach farther out to catch the ball than right-handed players, who wear their glove on the left hand. The extra couple of inches can make the difference between an out and a runner getting safely to first.

First Responsibilities

The first baseman has to stand far enough from the hitter to field—or get control of—a hit, but close enough to first base to get there quickly. If he fields the ball, he can run back to first or throw the ball to a pitcher who has come over to cover first base. Or, he might throw to another base for an out before moving back to first base to try for a double play.

After fielding a hit, St. Louis Cardinals first baseman Albert Pujols must make it to first base before the runner does to get an out.

19

It's the second baseman's responsibility to chase balls hit low between second base and the first baseman. Once he has the ball, he can start a double play by tossing it to the shortstop who's moved over to cover second base. Or, he can make an easy toss to first to get the batter out. He may even have time to step on the bag or tag a runner himself. If there are runners on base before the ball is hit, he'll also have to cover force-outs at second base.

Aaron Hill, second baseman for the Toronto Blue Jays, helps make a stunning double play against the Texas Rangers.

The shortstop is positioned between second and third base. It's one of the most active positions in baseball. The shortstop must be ready to field many hits during the game and quickly throw to any base. He backs up the second or third baseman during hits to those players. Deep balls hit to the outfield are often thrown to the shortstop to make sure runners can't advance too many bases.

Hanley Ramirez of the Florida Marlins makes a spectacular catch at shortstop.

Second Guessing

The second baseman and the shortstop share responsibilities for the middle of the field. Either player can cover second base depending on where the ball is hit. The two also back each other up to keep hit or thrown balls from going into the outfield.

The Arizona Diamondbacks' Mark Reynolds makes a throw from third base to put the hitter out at first base.

Third Base

Third basemen usually have to deal with two kinds of hits: hard line drives or slow balls along the baseline. Either way, the third baseman must move fast to get the ball before making a long, difficult throw to another base. Like the other infielders, the third baseman must try to force out or tag out runners coming his way. If runners make it safely to third, their next stop is home plate, where they will score a run.

22

Shutting Down Runners

Once one or more runners are on base, the infield's first job is to stop them from scoring. Throwing the batter out at first takes second place. Following a hit, the defense usually throws the ball to the infielder who can tag or force out the lead runner. If they're quick enough, the team can link several throws together for multiple outs on the same play.

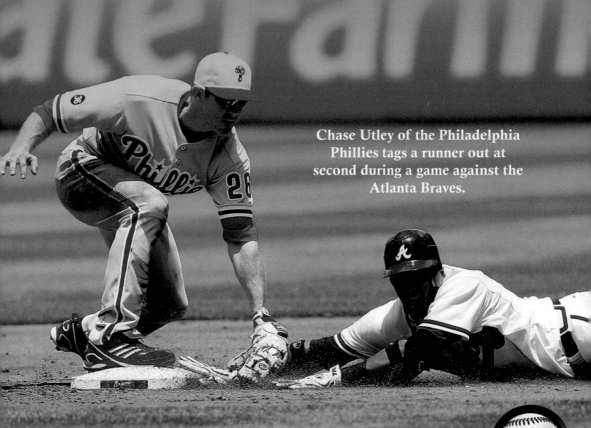

Chase Utley of the Philadelphia Phillies tags a runner out at second during a game against the Atlanta Braves.

23

KEY SKILLS

All infielders share certain skills. Here's what infielders do to cover all the bases.

Ready Position

Infielders give themselves the best chance to field hits by using the proper **stance**. Infielders prepare for hits with their knees bent, their feet shoulder width apart, and their weight on the balls of their feet. As soon as the pitcher begins to throw, an infielder draws his hands near the middle of his chest and begins moving forward. Infielders move as the batter swings because it's easier to react to a ball while in motion than while standing still.

Detroit Tigers first baseman Miguel Cabrera prepares to make a play just as the batter hits the ball.

An infielder may have less than a second to get his body or glove in front of a hit ball. To throw runners out, an infielder may have to leap up, dive to the side, kneel on the ground, run backward, or charge in for a ball as quickly as possible.

After forcing an out on third base, the New York Mets' David Wright throws the ball to second base to complete a double play against the San Diego Padres.

The Double Play

Even when an infielder catches the ball for an out, he must think and move fast. If a runner leaves a base before the hit is caught, he must go back to the base, which is known as tagging up. Getting the ball to an infielder on the base before the runner tags up gives the defense another out and a double play.

25

Troy Tulowitzki of the Colorado Rockies throws a runner out at first after a barehand catch.

Good Hands

Infielders must catch and handle balls without dropping them. Catching the ball in the glove is only the beginning of a defensive play. An infielder must quickly transfer the ball to his other hand to throw it. Sometimes an infielder doesn't have time to use his glove. To save time, he might "**barehand**" the ball before throwing.

Courage Under Fire

Making a quick, **accurate** throw is hard enough, but it can be even harder with a runner sprinting straight at you! Infielders trying to turn a double play must be brave enough to catch and throw from the base knowing that a runner will probably run or slide into them.

Accurate Throws

Brandon Phillips of the Cincinnati Reds gets hit hard by a runner at second. However, Phillips was able to complete the double play.

Infielders need to make hard, accurate throws, often with little time to wind up or aim. If an infielder jumps up or takes a couple of steps to catch a badly thrown ball, his foot will be off the base. The runner might then reach the base safely before the infielder can come back to the bag.

NO STEALING

A runner on base doesn't need to wait until the batter hits the ball to try to reach the next base. If the ball gets loose or the defense isn't paying attention, the runner can steal a base by running to it before being tagged out. Infielders must work hard to stop the other team from advancing bases on steals.

The Low Down

To increase his chances of stealing a base, the runner takes off as the pitcher begins throwing. The catcher has seconds to catch and throw the ball to the infielder. Since the infielder has to tag out a runner on a steal, he must make the catch and get the ball down to block the base and tag the sliding runner's foot.

The New York Yankees' Alex Rodriguez gets down low to catch a pass from the catcher and stop the runner from stealing third base.

Infielders can keep runners from stealing a base by standing on or near the runner's base. Runners often increase their chances of stealing a base by **leading off**. A runner who's leading off risks being thrown out if the pitcher decides to throw to the baseman instead of pitching. A runner unable to get back to base can get stuck in a **rundown** between two infielders. The infielders trap the runner between them by passing the ball back and forth until they can tag him out.

Joe Morgan

Joe Morgan

Cincinnati Reds second baseman Joe Morgan excelled at guessing when runners might steal. Morgan—who stole 692 bases himself—knew the signs. Morgan's skill and quickness helped him and Reds catcher Johnny Bench become a highly effective steal-stopping duo.

29

RELY ON THE RELAY

Infielders are the gateway between home plate and the outfield. Any balls they can't stop from reaching the outfield will be coming back soon enough. Infielders need to be able to catch a ball from the outfield and relay it quickly to another infielder to make outs.

The Cutoff

A batted ball that hits the ground in the outfield usually results in a base hit. In many situations, the outfielder won't be able to get the ball to first base in time. Furthermore, a hurried throw can go wild, allowing the runner to make it to second base. Instead, the outfielder throws the ball to the infielder protecting the base the runner would go to next. This play is called a "cutoff" because it keeps batters from getting extra bases.

Chicago White Sox shortstop Alexei Ramirez prepares to cover second base during a hit to the outfield.

Throwing Home

The relay throw is most important when an outfielder tries to get the ball to home plate in time to prevent a run. Few outfielders are strong and accurate enough to throw a ball all the way to home plate. It's faster to throw it to an infielder half the distance away who can then turn and hurl the ball to the catcher.

Texas Ranger Ian Kinsler relays a ball from the outfield to the catcher at home plate.

BEFORE THE GAME

Some of an infielder's most important preparation consists of learning where he needs to be and what he needs to do in every situation. This can change with each batter, each runner, and even each pitch!

Follow the Bouncing Ball

Through lots of practice, infielders can learn how a ball is likely to bounce or hop as it moves along the ground. Infielders practice fielding **ground balls** to get faster at making outs. In practice, coaches hit dozens of ground balls for infielders to go after, scoop up, and throw.

Philadelphia Phillies first baseman Ryan Howard prepares to catch a hopping ground ball.

Know Your Batter

Infielders judge where to wait for the hit by studying the other team's batters. If the infielders know that a batter tends to hit to the right, the shortstop might move closer to second base to allow the second baseman to field the ball.

The Playbook

Every infielder has a job to do on every play: go for the ball, cover a base, or back up another player. Infielders have to learn what to do in every situation. Knowing where to go and where to throw the ball on any given play will get outs and prevent runs.

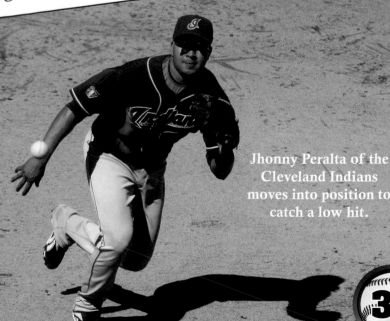

Jhonny Peralta of the Cleveland Indians moves into position to catch a low hit.

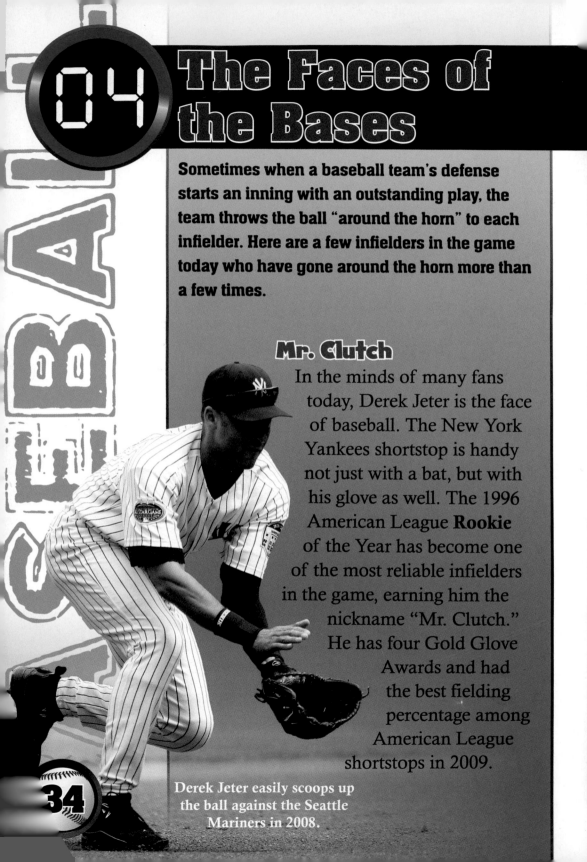

Sometimes when a baseball team's defense starts an inning with an outstanding play, the team throws the ball "around the horn" to each infielder. Here are a few infielders in the game today who have gone around the horn more than a few times.

Mr. Clutch

In the minds of many fans today, Derek Jeter is the face of baseball. The New York Yankees shortstop is handy not just with a bat, but with his glove as well. The 1996 American League **Rookie** of the Year has become one of the most reliable infielders in the game, earning him the nickname "Mr. Clutch." He has four Gold Glove Awards and had the best fielding percentage among American League shortstops in 2009.

Derek Jeter easily scoops up the ball against the Seattle Mariners in 2008.

Joining Jeter in the Yankees infield is first baseman Mark Teixeira. Teixeira, a three-time Gold Glove winner, helped form a defense that led to a World Series Championship in 2009. Teixeira doesn't just catch everything that comes to first base. He also makes hard, accurate throws to put out runners at other bases. His ability to knock down and control balls hit hard down the line disappoints many batters who watch Teixeira trot to first with the ball before they arrive.

Mark Teixeira is ready to catch the ball for an out against the Texas Rangers in 2010.

Kevin Youkilis grabs
a ground ball in a
game against the
Seattle Mariners.

First Among First Basemen

Most first basemen are happy to go a month
without making an **error**. The Red Sox's Kevin
Youkilis went error-free for a whole season in 2007.
Youkilis played 238 regular season games in a
row without an error—a record for first basemen.
His perfect season in 2007 was capped by his first
Gold Glove Award and a second World Series
Championship in 4 years with the Red Sox.

When Kevin Kouzmanoff joined the Oakland Athletics in 2010, the A's were looking for someone who could take over at third for Eric Chavez. Although Chavez won six straight Gold Glove Awards from 2001 to 2006, he became too injured to play. Kouzmanoff was a perfect choice for the team's "defense first" **strategy**. With the San Diego Padres, Kouzmanoff had just set a National League record for fielding percentage by a third baseman!

Kevin Kouzmanoff catches a ball in a game against the Los Angeles Angels of Anaheim.

Lifetime Achievement

Omar Vizquel has the best fielding percentage of any shortstop in history (.985). He has also helped make more double plays than any other shortstop. Vizquel has even played more games than any other shortstop. His impressive play has earned him 11 Gold Glove Awards, one of the highest totals ever.

"O" Wow!

Second baseman Orlando Hudson plays every game knowing he'll probably end up bruised. Hudson dives to the ground and stops line drives with his body. He makes perfect throws to first base even as runners slam into him. Hudson's rugged play has made him a four-time Gold Glove winner since 2005.

Orlando Hudson

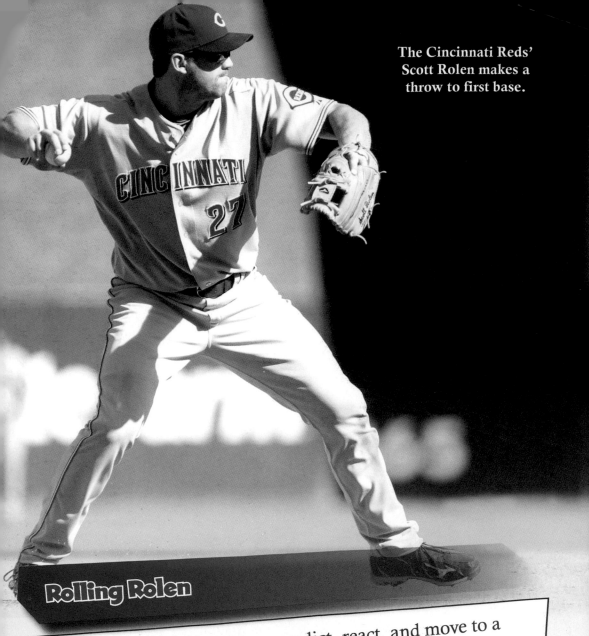

The Cincinnati Reds' Scott Rolen makes a throw to first base.

Rolling Rolen

Scott Rolen has the ability to predict, react, and move to a hit ball as well as anyone in baseball. The way he scoops up ground balls or pulls line drives out of the air makes him one of the best third basemen of all time. Rolen has earned seven Gold Gloves. Mike Schmidt and Brooks Robinson are the only third basemen to have earned more Gold Glove Awards, which puts Rolen in pretty good company.

Future Star: You!

Are you looking to become a star infielder? Try these exercises to help you cover the "base"-ics!

Grounders

To field a ball rolling or bouncing along the ground, get in front of it as quickly as possible. Set your feet in a wide stance, bend your knees, and put your glove down low near the ground. Keep your eye on the ball as it approaches. The path the ball is following should travel between your feet, right into your glove. Use your bare hand to trap the ball in the glove right away. Keep your body in front of the ball at all times to stop it in case it bounces or hops.

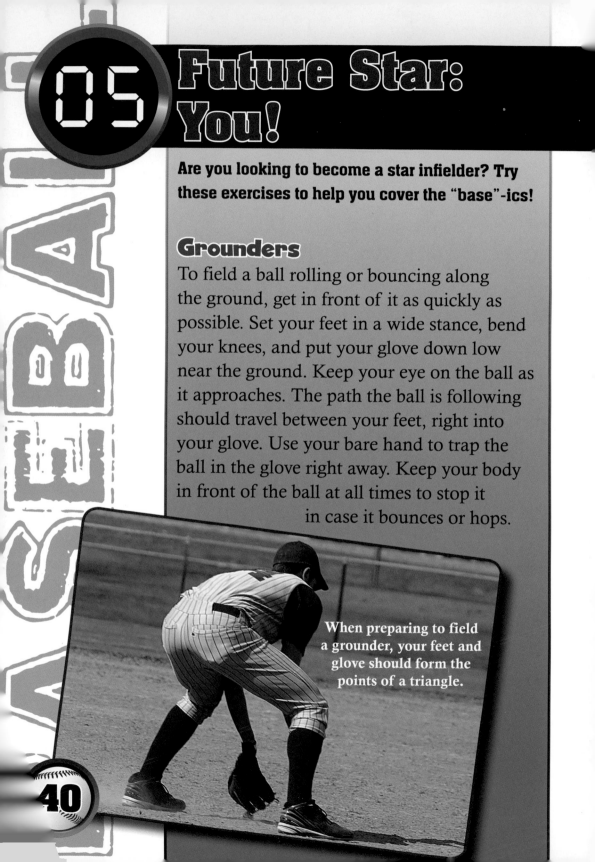

When preparing to field a grounder, your feet and glove should form the points of a triangle.

Even if a pop fly goes foul, catching it will still result in an out.

Pop-Ups

A high fly ball to the infield—called a pop fly—should be an easy catch, but you have to do it right. Quickly get under and slightly behind the spot where the ball will land. Tell your teammates that you have the ball so they don't run into you. Hold your glove just above your head and a little in front. Watch the ball as it falls into your glove. Squeeze the ball tight as it hits the webbing. Use your other hand to trap the ball in your glove.

Infielders need to make quick, accurate throws in order to make plays. With your throwing hand on the ball in your glove, turn your body so that your opposite shoulder points at your target. Place your throwing-side foot behind you, bringing your weight back, and pull the ball out of the glove. Your thumb should be below the ball, and your pointer and middle fingers should be on top as you bring the ball near your ear. Shift your weight forward. Step into the throw with your opposite foot. Make the throw, snapping your wrist as you release. Aim for your receiver's chest.

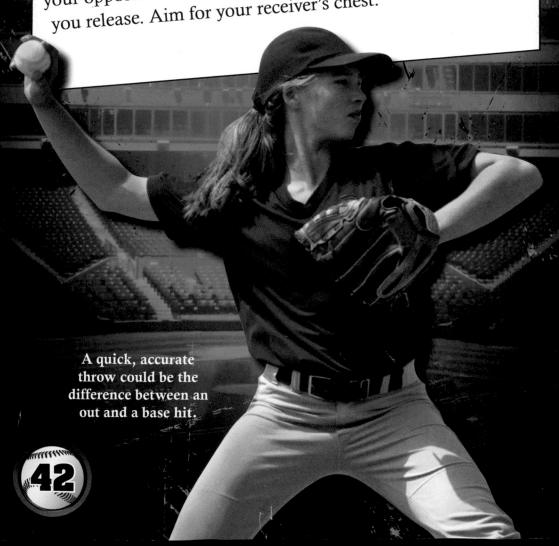

A quick, accurate throw could be the difference between an out and a base hit.

To practice receiving bad throws, have a partner throw off target on purpose or throw with the hand opposite the one he usually uses. For high throws, try to reach the ball while leaving one foot on the bag. For low throws, keep one foot on base while moving with your body to stay in front of the ball. Try to scoop up the ball with your glove, and remember to use both hands to hold it tight.

Accurate throws are important, but bad throws happen. It's important to know how to react to a bad throw.

43

Record Book

There are many ways to measure greatness. Here are a few ways to determine which infielders are the greatest at what they do.

Highest Career Fielding Percentage for an Infielder:

1. Casey Kotchman *(still active)* 1B .9982 *(as of 9/24/10)*
2. Kevin Youkilis *(still active)* 1B .9973 *(as of 9/24/10)*
3. Travis Lee 1B .9967
4. Mark Teixeira *(still active)* 1B .9964 *(as of 9/24/10)*
5. Doug Mientkiewicz 1B .9963

Highest Season Fielding Percentage for an Infielder:

1. Ten Players (listed by year) 1.000

Eddie Waitkus	1B	1954
Mike Hegan	1B	1971
Jason Thompson	1B	1980
Steve Garvey	1B	1984
Bob Horner	1B	1985
Luis Gonzalez	2B	2005
Wes Helms	1B	2006
Placido Polanco	2B	2007
Kevin Youkilis *(still active)*	1B	2007
Casey Kotchman *(still active)*	1B	2009

Casey Kotchman

Stan Musiel

Most Seasons with Highest Fielding Percentage for an Infielder:

1. Brooks Robinson	3B	11
2. Lou Boudreau	SS	10
3. Bid McPhee	2B	9
4. Eddie Collins	2B	8
Ozzie Smith	SS	8

Most Double Plays Made by Infield in a Season:

1. Philadelphia A's	217	1949
2. Pittsburgh Pirates	215	1966
3. New York Yankees	214	1956
4. Philadelphia A's	208	1950
5. Boston Red Sox	207	1949

Most Gold Glove Awards Received by an Infielder:

1. Brooks Robinson	3B	16
2. Ozzie Smith	SS	13
3. Keith Hernandez	1B	11
Omar Vizquel	SS	11
5. Roberto Alomar	2B	10
Mike Schmidt	3B	10

Most All-Star Appearances by an Infielder:

1. Stan Musiel	1B	24
2. Cal Ripken Jr.	SS	19
3. Rod Carew	1B/2B	18
Brooks Robinson	3B	18
5. Ozzie Smith	SS	15

Glossary

accurate: on target

barehand: to pick up or catch a ball without using a glove

defense: the team trying to stop the other team from scoring

double play: a situation where two outs result from a hit ball

error: a defensive mistake in handling a ball that allows a runner to get on base

fair ball: a ball hit off the bat that stays between the baseline from home plate to first base and the baseline from home plate to third base

fielding percentage: a measure of a fielder's ability, determined by dividing the fielder's putouts and assists by total number of putouts, assists, and errors

force-out: an out made by having control of the baseball and making contact with a base to which a runner must go before the runner makes contact

Gold Glove: an award given each year to the player with the highest fielding percentage at each defensive position in each league

ground ball: a hit ball that bounces along the ground

induct: to officially list a player in the Hall of Fame

inning: a unit of play where each baseball team gets a chance to bat until three outs have occurred. A professional baseball game has nine innings.

leading off: taking a few steps off the base toward the next base before the ball is pitched

line drive: a hard-hit ball that travels in a straight line

relay: a combination of throws from one player to another

rookie: a player in his first year playing a sport

rundown: a situation in which a runner is caught between bases by two infielders who pass the ball back and forth between them until the runner can be tagged out or gets safely to a base

stance: the way a player stands

strategy: a carefully thought-out plan

tag: to touch a player with the baseball or with the glove holding the baseball

triple play: a situation where three outs result from a hit ball

Books

Dreier, David. *Baseball: How It Works.* Mankato, MN: Capstone Press, 2010.

Glaser, Jason. *Jackie Robinson: Baseball's Great Pioneer.* Mankato, MN: Capstone Press, 2006.

Jacobs, Greg. *The Everything Kids' Baseball Book.* Avon, MA: Adams Media, 2010.

Kelley, James. *Baseball.* New York, NY: DK Publishing, 2010.

Lupica, Mike. *The Big Field.* New York, NY: Philomel Books, 2008.

Preller, James. *Six Innings.* New York, NY: Square Fish Books, 2010.

Web Sites

Club MLB
web.clubmlb.com
Major League Baseball's activity-filled site has games and interactive fun features to teach kids about baseball and its past and present players.

Kids' Club
mlb.mlb.com/mlb/kids/index.jsp
Major League Baseball's information site for kids who want to learn more about how to be a better player or want to write to their favorite player. The site also provides links to the pages of each Major League Baseball team.

National Baseball Hall of Fame
baseballhall.org
The Web site for the National Baseball Hall of Fame in Cooperstown, New York, tells the in-depth history of the game. Learn about the achievements of some of the finest players and personalities from more than 200 hundred years of baseball.

Index

About the Author

Jason Glaser is a freelance writer and stay-at-home father living in Mankato, Minnesota. He has written over fifty nonfiction books for children, including books on sports stars such as Jackie Robinson. As a youngster playing youth baseball, he once completed an unassisted triple play, which is the highlight of his sports career.